YOUR PASSPORT TO

KENYA

by Kaitlyn Duling

CONTENT CONSULTANT

Kefa M. Otiso, PhD
Professor of Geography
Director of the Global Village
College of Arts and Sciences
Bowling Green State University

CAPSTONE PRESS
a capstone imprint

Capstone Captivate is published by Capstone Press, an imprint of Capstone.
1710 Roe Crest Drive
North Mankato, Minnesota 56003
www.capstonepub.com

Library of Congress Cataloging-in-Publication Data
Names: Duling, Kaitlyn, author.
Title: Your passport to Kenya / Kaitlyn Duling.
Description: North Mankato, Minnesota : Capstone Press, 2021. | Series: World
  passport | Includes bibliographical references and index. | Audience:
  Grades 4-6
Identifiers: LCCN 2020001033 (print) | LCCN 2020001034 (ebook) | ISBN
  9781496684073 (hardcover) | ISBN 9781496687999 (paperback) | ISBN
  9781496684585 (pdf)
Subjects: LCSH: Kenya--Description and travel--Juvenile literature.
Classification: LCC DT433.522 .D84 2021 (print) | LCC DT433.522 (ebook) |
  DDC 967.62--dc23
LC record available at https://lccn.loc.gov/2020001033
LC ebook record available at https://lccn.loc.gov/2020001034

Image Credits
AP Images: Kike Calvo, 9; iStockphoto: FernandoQuevedo, 23; Red Line Editorial: 5; Shutterstock Images: Byelikova Oksana, 20, Dmitry Burlakov, 17, Jen Watson, 19, Jlwarehouse, 27, Julinzy, cover (flag), Martin Mwaura, 13, mbrand85, 15, Natashadub, cover (map), photocosmos1, 28, Piu_Piu, 6, Volodymyr Burdiak, cover (bottom), 16
Design Elements: iStockphoto, Shutterstock Images

Editorial Credits
Editor: Jamie Hudalla; Designer: Colleen McLaren

All internet sites appearing in back matter were available and accurate when this book was sent to press.

Printed in the United States of America.
PA117

CONTENTS

Words in **bold** are in the glossary.

CHAPTER ONE

WELCOME TO KENYA!

The narrow streets of Nairobi are crowded. Buses honk. Bikes zoom past. The air is full of yummy smells, such as cooked meat and fried donuts. At the edge of Kenya's capital, elephants wander in a huge national park. Lions nap in the shade. Past the park, there are villages. Children walk to school. Adults farm the fields.

Kenya is in East Africa. It shares borders with Ethiopia, Somalia, South Sudan, Tanzania, and Uganda. Its eastern edge touches the Indian Ocean. From wide **savannas** to tall mountain peaks, the country has many beautiful sites. In recent years, the population has grown quickly. There are now more than 50 million people. Many are moving from the countryside to the cities.

MAP OF KENYA

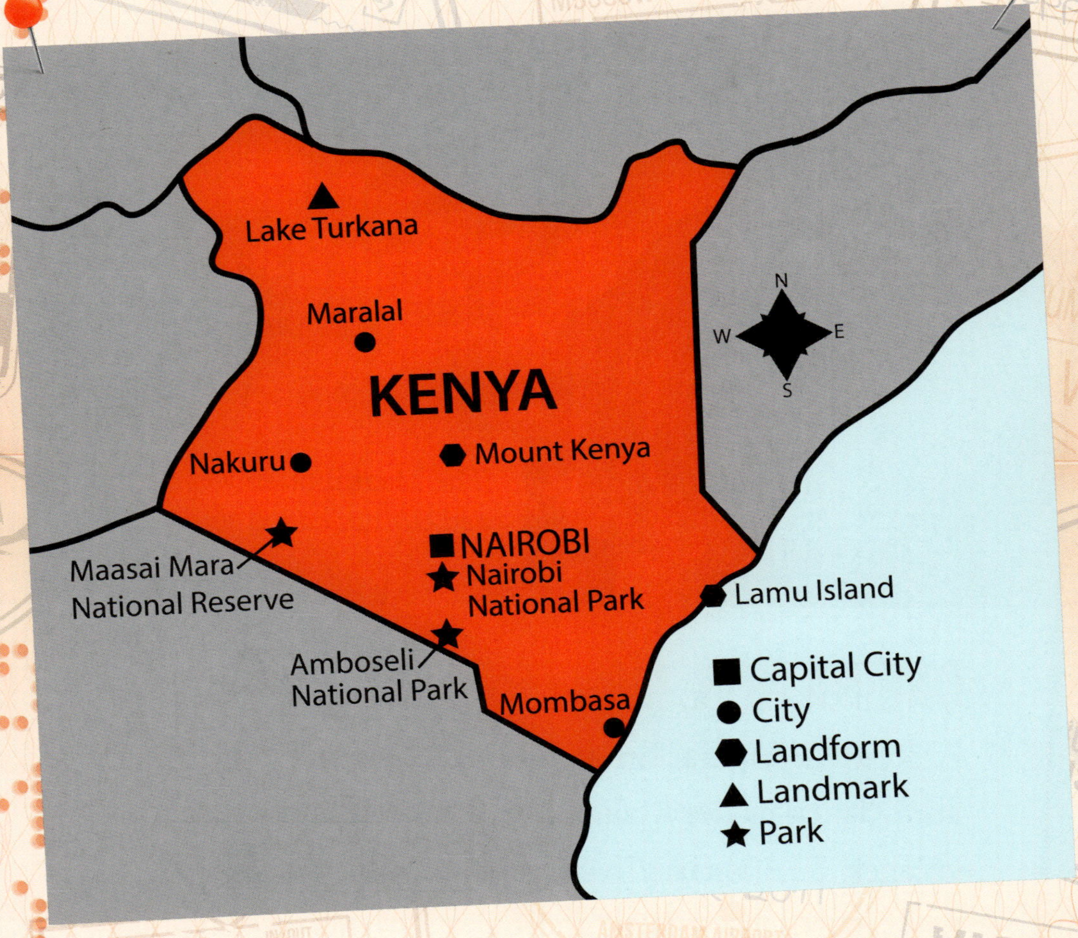

Lake Turkana

Maralal

KENYA

Nakuru

Mount Kenya

■ NAIROBI
★ Nairobi
National Park

Maasai Mara
National Reserve

Amboseli
National Park

Mombasa

Lamu Island

■ Capital City
● City
⬡ Landform
▲ Landmark
★ Park

N
W   E
S

Explore Kenya's
cities and landmarks.

The Maasai often wear red clothes called *shukas*.

ONE NATION, MANY PEOPLE

Kenya's population includes many **ethnic groups**. Some, such as the Maasai and Turkana, live in small villages. The Maasai live in southern Kenya. They raise livestock for food and for sale. Many are strong warriors. Maasai wear red cotton clothes called *shukas*, which is a Swahili word. Swahili is one of Kenya's main languages.

FACT FILE

OFFICIAL NAME: .... REPUBLIC OF KENYA
POPULATION: 53,527,936
LAND AREA: .... 219,746 SQ. MI. (569,140 SQ KM)
CAPITAL: .... NAIROBI
MONEY: .... KENYAN SHILLING (KES)
GOVERNMENT: .... PRESIDENTIAL REPUBLIC
LANGUAGE: .... SWAHILI, OR KISWAHILI, AND ENGLISH
GEOGRAPHY: Kenya is located in Eastern Africa and borders the Indian Ocean. The country shares land borders with Ethiopia, Somalia, South Sudan, Tanzania, and Uganda.
NATURAL RESOURCES: Kenya has gemstones such as sapphires and rubies. It also has limestone, salt, oil, and hydropower, which is energy that comes from water.

The Turkana live in northwest Kenya. They raise camels and cattle. People from Europe, South Asia, and other parts of Africa live in the urban city areas of Kenya.

Music and storytelling are important in Kenya. Ethnic groups have long used songs, poems, and stories to pass down their knowledge, beliefs, and **customs**.

CHAPTER TWO

HISTORY OF KENYA

People have lived in the land that is now Kenya for millions of years. Fossils of early human bones and tools have been found in Kenya. People started moving to the area around the year 2000 **BCE**. They came from other parts of Africa.

The first Kenyans hunted for and gathered food. They moved around to find food. Some later began to keep livestock, such as sheep, goats, and camels. In the 400s **CE**, Arab settlers moved into the coastal areas. They traded with Persia and India for ivory, rhino horns, gold, and shells. These things were very valuable. Many people came to Kenya to trade for these items.

FIGHTING FOR CONTROL

The Arab settlers took control of the Kenyan coast and its people. They also influenced Kenyan culture. Swahili borrows many words from Arabic.

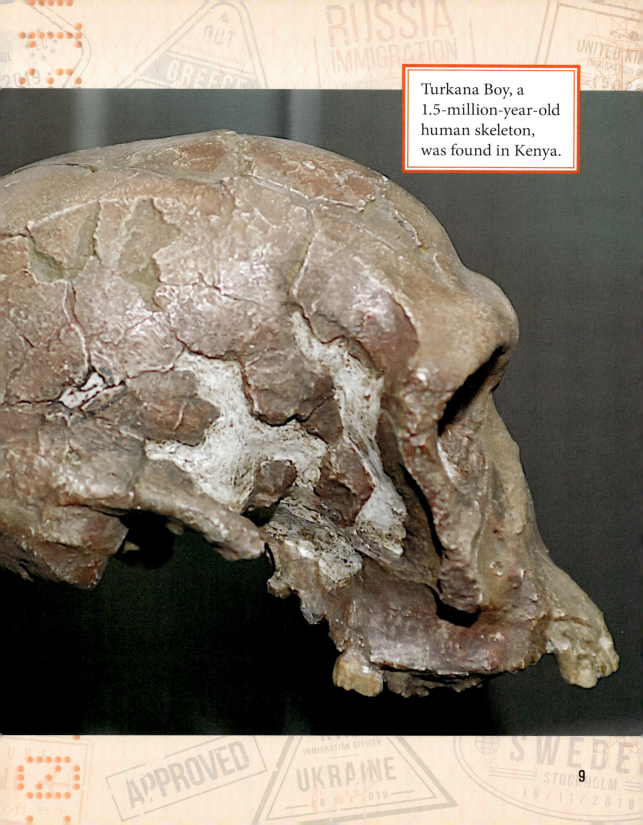

Turkana Boy, a 1.5-million-year-old human skeleton, was found in Kenya.

TIMELINE OF KENYAN HISTORY

400: Arabs settle in the coastal areas and develop trade stations.

1498: Portuguese explorers arrive in Kenya.

1505: The Portuguese and Arabs from the Middle East go to war over control of the region of Kenya.

1580s: The Portuguese defeat the Turks in a fight to control the region. The Portuguese continue to fight the Arabs. After 100 years, the Arabs win.

1895: Kenya becomes a British colony. Shortly after, British settlers move into the highlands.

1952: A group known as the Mau Mau begins fighting British settlers to protect their land.

1963: Kenya gains **independence** from Britain.

1978: Daniel arap Moi becomes president. He holds office for 24 years until 2002.

2010: A new set of laws is approved. It limits the powers of the president. The president can serve up to two terms of 5 years each.

In 1498, Portuguese explorers arrived on the Kenyan coast. They wanted to use trade routes on the Indian Ocean. The Portuguese gained power over the Kenyan coast. About 100 years later, the Islamic leader of Oman tried to do the same. For nearly 400 years, the Portuguese, Arabs, and Turks all fought for control of Kenya.

INDEPENDENCE

In 1895, the British **colonized** Kenya. British and Indian settlers moved in. Britain also ruled India.

The British did not let most Kenyans participate in politics. The Kenyans had no power over their own region. In 1952, they rebelled against the British. They fought to gain control over their government. Kenya finally gained independence in 1963.

Kenya's government is now a presidential **republic**. Daniel arap Moi was president from 1978 to 2002. In 2010, Kenya passed a set of laws. Those laws limited the power of the president. The country now elects a president every five years.

FACT

In 2018, Kenya was the fourth-largest producer of flowers. Roses, lilies, and other flowers are grown in Kenya. They are sold around the world.

CHAPTER THREE

EXPLORE KENYA

There is beauty everywhere in Kenya. Visitors can explore tall mountains and deep valleys. There are flat savannas and sandy beaches. Coffee and tea farms stretch out across the rural countryside.

NATURAL SITES

Tourism is very important in Kenya. It brings in a lot of money. People travel from all over the world to visit the country. They go on wildlife **safaris** in Kenya's nature parks. The parks are full of large wild animals. Visitors can spot lions, elephants, and more.

Mount Kenya is the second-highest mountain in Africa. It is a popular site. The mountain is a volcano. It no longer erupts. The Kikuyu people live at the base of the mountain. They believe that it is the home of Ngai, their god.

People can hike
Mount Kenya.

CITIES TO VISIT

Kenya has large cities. Nairobi is the largest. Its name means "cold water" in the local Maasai language. There are houses and skyscrapers. More than 4 million people live there. Animals live there too. Nairobi National Park is inside the city limits. It is just 4 miles (6.4 kilometers) from the city center. A fence separates the lions, rhinos, and other animals from the city. Tourists also love to visit the city's museums. The Nairobi National Museum highlights Kenya's nature, history, and art.

MOMBASA

Mombasa is the country's oldest and second-largest city. It was founded in 900 CE. More than 1 million people lived there as of 2016. It is on the edge of the Indian Ocean. Mombasa has the largest **port** in East Africa. It has long been a big trading center. Today, tourists from across the globe travel to the city. They enjoy its beautiful beaches and fancy hotels. Visitors can get to the city from Nairobi by train. They can see animals when the train passes through Tsavo National Park and Nairobi National Park.

Nairobi National Park is home to many wild animals.

Nakuru is another big city. People from Africa, Europe, and Asia live there. The city is famous for its flamingos. Thousands of these pink birds live at Lake Nakuru.

Mount Kilimanjaro is the tallest mountain in Africa.

PARKS AND RESERVES

Kenya is full of wildlife outside its cities. In 1946, the country made its first national park. Today, there are 55 national parks and game reserves. Visitors can go on safaris to see large animals in the wild. The most famous park is the Maasai Mara National Reserve. There, people can see lions, leopards, buffalos, rhinos, and elephants.

While in national parks, visitors must stop for animals crossing the road.

Visitors to Amboseli National Park get another amazing view. From the park, they can see Mount Kilimanjaro. It is the largest mountain in Africa. This mountain sits on the border of Kenya and Tanzania.

CHAPTER FOUR

DAILY LIFE

Most Kenyans are farmers. They grow crops such as corn. Farmers also raise cows and goats. They use most of the food they grow and raise to feed their families. Some farmers sell their food. Most people in rural areas cook their food using firewood. Water for cooking and bathing usually comes from nearby wells and rivers. Some groups, such as the Maasai, eat meat and drink milk from their cattle.

VILLAGES AND CITIES

The El Molo tribe is one of the smallest in Kenya. They live in a village on the shore of Lake Turkana. Their homes are huts made of reeds. They use spears and nets to catch fish on the lake. The El Molo also hunt hippos and crocodiles. Women weave baskets and make jewelry. There are villages like this one across Kenya. Each village has unique music, dances, clothing, and food. Some have their own languages too.

Some Kenyans grow and sell tea leaves.

The El Molo construct their homes out of reeds.

Most people live in rural areas, but cities are now growing. In Nairobi, many people work in offices. They ride buses, cars, and trains to work. Some children ride bikes and buses to school. On weekends, many families gather. They eat meals and go to church.

COMMON MEALS

Breakfast is usually a cup of tea or corn porridge with bread or potatoes. One popular Kenyan food is *chapati*. This is a flat wheat bread. *Ugali* is also common. It is a cornmeal mash.

Ugali is usually eaten with spiced vegetables or meat stews. Stew vegetables often include spinach. Meat from cattle and goats is also popular. British, Arab, and Indian foods have influenced Kenyan cooking. So Kenyans eat rice, chilies, and curries. Kenyans also love juicy fruits, such as mangoes and coconuts. Special occasions are a time for *nyama choma*. That is Swahili for "roast meat."

UGALI

Ugali is a stiff corn mash often served with meat or vegetables. Kenyans usually eat ugali with their hands. They use it to scoop up and eat a small portion of a vegetable or meat stew. With the help of an adult, you can make this recipe at home.

Ugali Ingredients:
- 4 cups of water
- 1 teaspoon of salt
- 2 cups of white cornmeal or millet

Ugali Directions:

1. Pour water and salt into a saucepan.
2. Bring the water to a boil. Slowly stir in the cornmeal.
3. Turn the heat to medium-low. Continue stirring, mashing lumps with a spoon. Do this for about 10 minutes.
4. The mush should be thick and pull away from the sides of the pot.
5. Remove from heat and allow to cool. After it cools, you can form the ugali into a ball and serve.

CHAPTER FIVE

HOLIDAYS AND CELEBRATIONS

There is no official religion in Kenya. However, most Kenyans are Christian. Islam is also widely practiced in Kenya. About 83 percent of Kenyans are Christian, and 11 percent are Muslim. About 2 percent practice African traditional religions, and another 2 percent are not religious. Both Christian and Muslim holy days are national holidays. They include Christmas and Eid al-Fitr. Kenyan schools and some businesses are closed for these holidays.

THE INTERNATIONAL CAMEL DERBY

Every year, people come from far and wide to watch the camel derby. The race begins just outside the town of Maralal. There are different distances for each camel race. The region's finest camels gather at the starting line. The animals run through the desert. Riders try to balance on top of the one-humped camels. Camels are not harmed during the race. Whoever finishes the race first is the winner!

Muslims worship in mosques such as Jamia Mosque in Nairobi.

CHAPTER SIX

SPORTS AND RECREATION

Many Kenyans love to watch and play soccer. They call it football. Kenyans also play rugby, cricket, and wrestling. Board games, such as mancala, are also popular. Mancala is a traditional East African board game. It is played with small stones on a long wooden board. In Kenya, the game is called *Bao*.

WINNING MEDALS

Kenyan athletes compete around the world. Since 1956, Kenya has sent athletes to nearly every Summer Olympics. Over the years, they have won more than 100 Olympic medals.

Kenyans often compete in track and field events. They have been successful in distance-running events. Kenyan athletes have won a few medals in boxing too.

Whether in cities or villages, kids in Kenya love to play football.

Eliud Kipchoge is one of the best long-distance runners in the world.

Some of the most successful long-distance runners are from Kenya. In 2019, Eliud Kipchoge became the world-record holder for the fastest time running a marathon. He ran a marathon in less than two hours!

FACT
|||||||||||||||||||||||||||||||||||||||||||||||||||||||||||||||

On October 13, 2019, Kenyan runner Brigid Kosgei won the Chicago Marathon. She set a new women's world record. She ran the race in 2 hours, 14 minutes, 4 seconds.

KOLOLO-I

In rural parts of Kenya, children may not have many toys or access to technology. They play games that use little or no equipment. To play *Kololo-i*, you will need six or more people and an open space.

1. Form a circle and join hands.
2. Move in a circle quickly while swinging hands.
3. One person chants these words: *Kololo-i howuee kanga*, which is similar to "Let's move."
4. The group chants these words: *Kololo-i howuee kanga.*
5. If two people drop hands at any point, they must leave the circle.
6. Two at a time must leave until only two people remain. Those two are the winners.

GLOSSARY

BCE/CE
BCE means Before Common Era, or before year one. CE means Common Era, or after year one

colonized (KAH-luh-nized)
settled in and took control of a foreign country

customs (KUHS-tuhms)
traditions specific to a place or group

diversity (dye-VUR-suh-tee)
a wide range of different people or things

ethnic groups (ETH-nik GROOPS)
people who share a common culture, race, language, or nationality

independence (in-di-PEN-duhnss)
the freedom a country has to govern itself

port (PORT)
a place where ships are loaded and unloaded

republic (ri-PUB-lik)
a type of government where people elect their political leaders and president

safaris (suh-FAH-rees)
journeys in which someone can witness animals in their natural habitat

savannas (suh-VAN-uhs)
grassy plains with very few trees

READ MORE

Klepeis, Alicia Z. *Kenya*. New York: Cavendish Square, 2018.

Rechner, Amy. *Kenya*. Minneapolis, MN: Bellwether Media, 2019.

Tanumihardja, Pat. *Amazing Mountains Around the World*. Mankato, MN: Capstone Press, 2019.

INTERNET SITES

National Geographic Kids: Kenya
https://kids.nationalgeographic.com/explore/countries/kenya

PBS Learning Media: Time for School | Kenya: Joab
https://whut.pbslearningmedia.org/resource/vtl07.la.rv.text
.kenyaclass/a-look-at-a-kenyan-classroom

Scholastic: Global Trek: Learn About Kenya
http://teacher.scholastic.com/activities/globaltrek
/destinations/popups/kenya.htm

INDEX

OTHER BOOKS IN THIS SERIES

YOUR PASSPORT TO CHINA
YOUR PASSPORT TO ECUADOR
YOUR PASSPORT TO EL SALVADOR
YOUR PASSPORT TO ETHIOPIA
YOUR PASSPORT TO FRANCE
YOUR PASSPORT TO IRAN
YOUR PASSPORT TO PERU
YOUR PASSPORT TO RUSSIA
YOUR PASSPORT TO SPAIN